INTRO TO CHEMISTRY Need to Know

SilverTip

Acids and Bases

by Daniel R. Faust

Consultant: Sara Vogt
Science Educator at Anoka Hennepin School District

BEARPORT
PUBLISHING

Minneapolis, Minnesota

Credits

Cover and title page, © Helin Loik-Tomson/iStock; 4, © Alex Staroseltsev/Shutterstock; 5T, © IgorZh/Shutterstock; 5B, © WilliamEdwards14/Shutterstock; 6, © khak/Shutterstock; 9, © OSweetNature/Shutterstock; 10, © Melica/Shutterstock; 13, © Ground Picture/Shutterstock; 15, © Dmitriy Rybin/Shutterstock; 16–17, © ESB Professional/Shutterstock; 19, © chemical industry/Shutterstock; 21T, © Ewa Studio/Shutterstock; 21B, © Kabachki.photo/Shutterstock; 22, © Ekkaphop/Shutterstock; 23, © H_Ko/Shutterstock; 25, © Olesya_sh/Shutterstock; 27, © ESB Professional/Shutterstock; and 28, © Inkoly/Shutterstock.

Bearport Publishing Company Product Development Team

President: Jen Jenson; Director of Product Development: Spencer Brinker; Senior Editor: Allison Juda; Editor: Charly Haley; Associate Editor: Naomi Reich; Senior Designer: Colin O'Dea; Associate Designer: Elena Klinkner; Associate Designer: Kayla Eggert; Product Development Assistant: Anita Stasson

Library of Congress Cataloging-in-Publication Data is available at www.loc.gov or upon request from the publisher.

ISBN: 979-8-88509-422-1 (hardcover)
ISBN: 979-8-88509-544-0 (paperback)
ISBN: 979-8-88509-659-1 (ebook)

Copyright © 2023 Bearport Publishing Company. All rights reserved. No part of this publication may be reproduced in whole or in part, stored in any retrieval system, or transmitted in any form or by any means, electronic, mechanical, photocopying, recording, or otherwise, without written permission from the publisher.

For more information, write to Bearport Publishing, 5357 Penn Avenue South, Minneapolis, MN 55419.

Contents

Kitchen Chemistry 4

Break It Down 6

All about Ions 10

Acidic or Basic? 12

Weak and Strong 16

What's Your Number? 20

Passing the Test 22

Universally Useful 24

Acids and Bases 28

SilverTips for Success 29

Glossary 30

Read More 31

Learn More Online 31

Index 32

About the Author 32

Kitchen Chemistry

Have you ever tasted a sour lemon? How about watched a cake with baking soda puff up in the oven? These things happen thanks to acids and bases in action.

Acids and bases are all around. To spot them, you just need to know what to look for.

Lemons taste sour because they have citric (SIT-rik) acid. It is an acid found in many citrus fruits. This gives orange juice its tart taste, too.

Break It Down

Most things are either acids or bases. What makes something one or the other? It has to do with the smallest parts of our universe.

Everything is made up of tiny **atoms**. Within each atom there are even smaller parts called protons and electrons.

Some things are not an acid or a base. If something does not have the **properties** of either, it is said to be **neutral**. Pure water is neutral.

A Model of an Atom

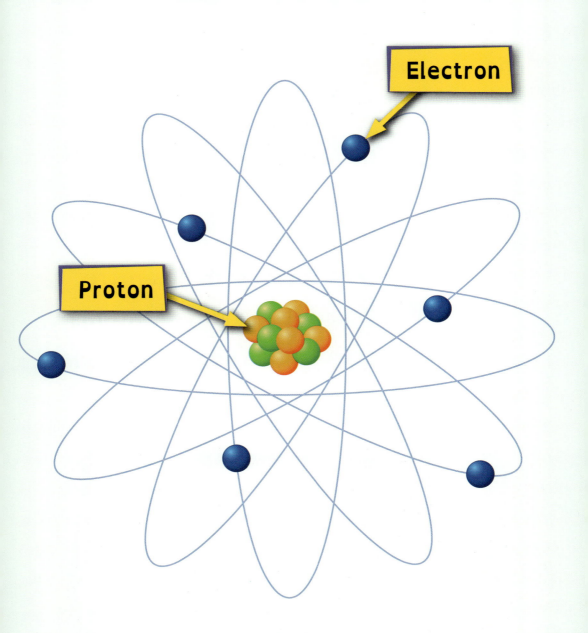

These parts of an atom have electric charges. Protons are positive, and electrons are negative.

Many atoms have the same number of protons and electrons. The charges cancel out, so most atoms have no charge. However, if an atom has more protons, it is positively charged. Atoms with more electrons are negative.

If two atoms have the same charge, they repel. They move away from each other. If they have different charges, they attract. That means they move toward each other.

Positive and negative charges in atoms work like the poles of a magnet.

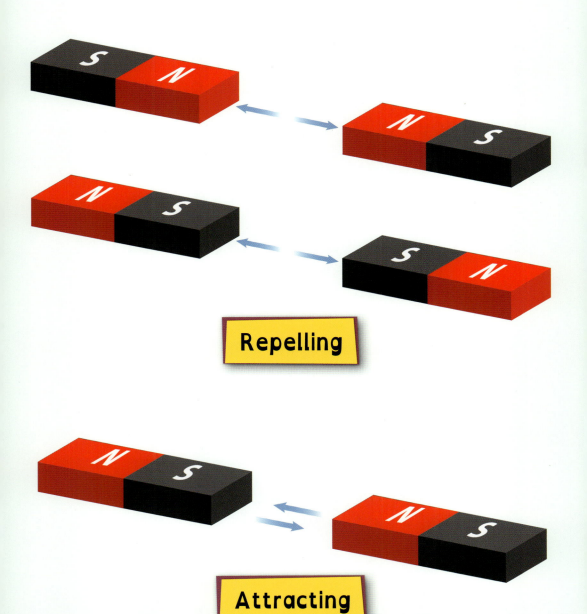

All about Ions

When an atom has a charge, it is called an **ion**. Ions can be positive or negative. What does all this have to do with acids and bases? Everything! An acid is something that makes hydrogen ions. A base is something that **absorbs** hydrogen ions.

When an acid and a base are mixed together, they cancel each other out. There is not a charge anymore. This process makes a kind of salt.

A balanced hydrogen atom

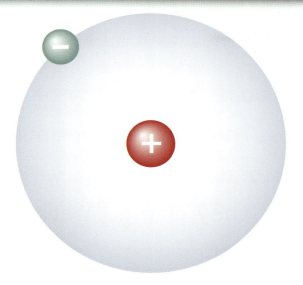

A positively-charged hydrogen ion

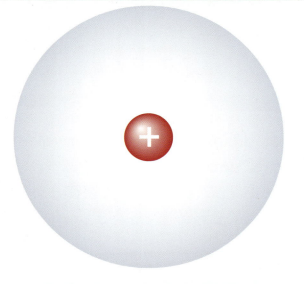

Hydrogen is an element.

Acidic or Basic?

Acids and bases have many of the same properties. They behave in similar ways. Both acids and bases **react** with metal. This means they change metal from one thing into another.

Acids and bases are also good **conductors**. Electricity moves through them easily.

Not all of the properties of acids and bases are easy to see. Some can only be spotted if the acid or base is mixed with water.

Because they are good conductors, acids and bases are used in batteries.

13

What's different about acids and bases? For one, they taste different. Remember that lemon? Its taste comes from citric acid. Acids are sour. They can also feel rough on your skin.

On the other hand, bases taste bitter. They have a slippery, slimy feel.

Tap water in some places is basic. Other places have more acidic water. This is called hard and soft water. A water softener can make hard water more neutral.

Weak and Strong

The strength of an acid or base has to do with the number of ions. When mixed with water, weak acids have fewer hydrogen ions than strong acids. Bases absorb hydrogen ions in water. The more ions a base absorbs, the stronger it is.

Strong acids and bases conduct electricity better than weak acids and bases. The acids and bases used in light bulbs are very strong.

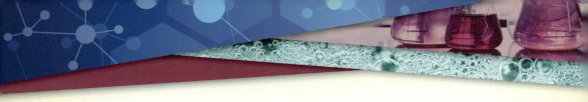

You may come across acids and bases every day. Many are pretty safe to be around. In fact, soap is a base that helps keep you safe by cleaning things.

However, some acids and bases can be very harmful. The stronger an acid or base is, the more dangerous it can be.

Strong acids and bases can burn your skin and sting your eyes. The strongest acids and bases can even make their way through skin and bones.

What's Your Number?

Scientists use the **pH scale** to measure the strength of acids and bases. The scale ranges from numbers 0 through 14. Acids are used for 0 through 6, with the lower numbers being more acidic. Bases are 8 through 14. Strong bases have a high pH.

The pH 7 is neutral. Things with this pH do not have the properties of acids or bases. Pure water is found at the middle of the pH scale.

Tomatoes have a pH of 4.

Milk is close to neutral. It is a 6.

Passing the Test

How can you find out just how acidic or basic something is? Scientists often use **litmus paper** (LIT-muhs PAY-pur). These paper strips have special dyes on them. Litmus paper can be blue, red, or purple. The paper changes color when it touches acids and bases.

The first dyes in litmus paper came from lichen (LYE-kuhn). This is a type of small plant that grows on trees, rocks, and walls.

Universally Useful

They're in everything from the soda you sip to the detergent you use to clean your dishes. It's hard to imagine a world without acids and bases. Acids are also used to make glass, plastic, rubber, and paper. Bases come in handy to create cement and even clothing.

Acids can kill the things that make food go bad. Vinegar is an acid that is used to make certain vegetables last longer. It adds a sour, acidic taste to the food.

There are even acids and bases inside of you! Without acids and bases your body would not be able to turn the food you eat into energy. Acids and bases in your stomach work together to break down food. They really are everywhere.

The acid in your stomach is very strong. If there is too much, you can feel sick. Taking an antacid may make you feel better. That's because it's a base.

Acids and Bases

Everything can be found somewhere along the pH scale. What can we expect from acids and bases depending on where they fall?

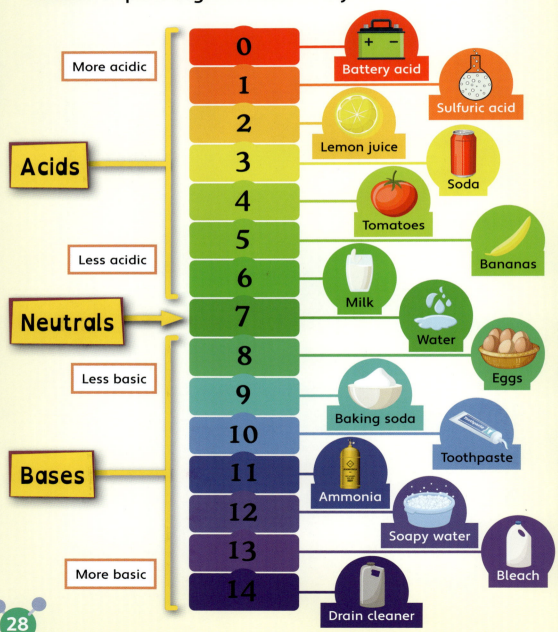

SilverTips for SUCCESS

⭐ SilverTips for REVIEW

Review what you've learned. Use the text to help you.

Define key terms

acid
base
ion

neutral
pH scale

Check for understanding

Describe the properties of acids and bases. What is the same and what is different about them?

How do ions make something an acid or a base?

What is the purpose of the pH scale, and how can it be tested?

Think deeper

Use your understanding of acids and bases to think of two things not mentioned in this book that are acids. Think of two more bases.

⭐ SilverTips on TEST-TAKING

- **Make a study plan.** Ask your teacher what the test is going to cover. Then, set aside time to study a little bit every day.

- **Read all the questions carefully.** Be sure you know what is being asked.

- **Skip any questions** you don't know how to answer right away. Mark them and come back later if you have time.

Glossary

absorbs takes in

atoms the tiny building blocks that make up every substance in the universe

conductors materials that allow heat or electricity to move through them

ion an atom with a positive or negative charge

litmus paper paper with dyes that change color in the presence of a base or an acid

neutral in the middle, without the properties of acids or bases

pH scale a measure that shows a range from acidic to basic

properties the ways things look or act

react to change after coming into contact with something

Read More

Ahrens, Niki. *Hack Your Kitchen: Discover a World of Food Fun with Science Buddies.* Minneapolis: Lerner Publications, 2021.

Griffin, Mary. *The pH Scale (A Look at Chemistry).* New York: Gareth Stevens Publishing, 2019.

Linde, Barbara M. *Makerspace Projects for Understanding Chemical Reactions (STEM Makerspace Projects).* New York: PowerKids Press, 2021.

Learn More Online

1. Go to **www.factsurfer.com** or scan the QR code below.
2. Enter "**Acids and Bases**" into the search box.
3. Click on the cover of this book to see a list of websites.

Index

atoms 6–11

conductors 12–13, 17

dangerous 18–19

electric charge 8–11

feel 14

hydrogen 10–11, 16

ion 10–11, 16

litmus paper 22

neutral 6, 20–21, 28

pH scale 20, 28

properties 6, 12, 20

reactive 12

safe 18

strength 16–18, 20, 26

taste 4, 14, 24

water 6, 12, 14, 16, 20, 28

About the Author

Daniel R. Faust is a freelance writer of fiction and nonfiction. He lives in Brooklyn, NY.